"Great book!! Greprocess. It is amaz... complicated and intimidating part of the justice system. Few resources are as clear and helpful, for plaintiffs and lawyers alike! Great job!!"

— Kristen West, Portland OR

"As both the daughter of a chiropractor and someone who has managed insurance claims for over 15 years, I am thankful that an effort is being made to respectfully inform auto accident victims of the snares and difficulties they may face during the course of their claim."

— Corrin Coker, Tualatin OR

"This book is great! You have found a good balance between complexity and accessibility. I really respect your effort to empower people when they engage in the legal system. This is something I strive to do with my clients and potential clients, but you have taken it to a much higher level."

— Benjamin Haile, Attorney, Portland OR

I found the book [7 Common Mistakes That Can Wreck Your Oregon Accident Case] to be very informative and easy to read. I felt it provided excellent information that would be helpful for a person injured in an automobile accident that is seeking compensation for injuries suffered from the accident. The book provides options to people and advice on how to pursue a claim.

— Don Menzia, Vancouver WA

7 Common Mistakes That Can Wreck Your Oregon Accident Case

JOSHUA SHULMAN AND SEAN DUBOIS
PARTNERS AT SHULMAN DUBOIS LLC

Copyright © 2012 by Shulman DuBois LLC
All rights reserved. No part of this book may be used or reproduced in any manner whatsoever without written permission by the authors.

Printed in the United States of America.

ISBN: 1475189540
ISBN: 978-1-47518-954-4

Don't Wreck Your Oregon Accident Claim

Have you been in accident? Gotten hurt and don't know what to do? Are you worried about paying increasing medical bills? Does the insurance adjustor keep calling? Or ignore your calls completely?

Then this book is for you.

If we can give you one suggestion about what to do after an accident, it is:

Educate yourself.

After seeing how the insurance industry can destroy the financial well-being of people who are in the claims process, we have made it our personal mission to protect injury victims and their families, and to force insurance companies to treat them fairly by paying fair compensation. We strongly believe that accident victims can maximize their financial recovery from the insurance companies by starting with a good understanding of the personal injury claims process.

Before you talk to an insurance company, or hire a lawyer, educate yourself. Do research. Search the web. Read this book. Read another book. Talk to friends who have hired lawyers. Contact a lawyer with questions. Educate yourself.

Brought to you by:
Shulman DuBois LLC
1553 SE Tolman St.
Portland, OR 97202
(503) 222-4411
www.PDXInjuryLaw.com
info@pdxinjurylaw.com

Seven Common Mistakes
That Can Wreck Your
Oregon Accident Case

Essential information you should
know before you hire a lawyer
or talk to the insurance company.

Insurance company wants to
"Ask you a few questions?"
Read this book first!

Joshua Shulman and Sean DuBois
Partners at Shulman DuBois LLC
In Portland, OR

Acknowledgements:

We would like to acknowledge the following people for their contributions to this edition. We could not have completed this project without the help of these professionals. Thank you all for the time and effort you put into this book.

Maureen Inouye
Amy Lynne Watson, DC
Benjamin Haile, Attorney at Law
Simon Agger, DC
Shelly Coffman, MPT, OCS, FAAOMPT, CSCS
Jerome Craig, DC, LMT, CSCS
Jason Lindekugel, DC
Sarah Hart
Corrin Coker

Contents

Foreword
    Who Should Read This Book? 1
    Why Should I Read This Book? 1
    Legal Disclaimer 2

Chapter 1
    7 Common Mistakes That Can Wreck Your
    Oregon Accident Case 3
        Should I Give a Recorded Statement? 4
        Car Crash or Car Accident? 12

Chapter 2
    7 Common Myths You May Have Heard From Friends,
    Relatives, or Well-Meaning Neighbors 15
        The McDonald's Coffee Case – A Myth Explained 20

Chapter 3
    What Is My Case Worth? 23
        How Bankruptcy Can Affect Your Personal Injury Case 26

Chapter 4
    "How Long Do I Have to File?": Oregon's Statutes of
    Limitations 27
        Statutes of Limitations You NEED to Know 28

Chapter 5
    Auto Insurance Policies – The Basics 31

Chapter 6
    Liability Insurance 35
        Insurance Policy Limits 36

Chapter 7
    Personal Injury Protection (PIP) 37

Chapter 8
    Underinsured Motorist Insurance (UIM) 41
        How Many Uninsured Drivers Are Out There? 43

Chapter 9
    Health Insurance – Your Last Resort 45

Chapter 10
    Medical Liens and the Importance of Negotiation 47

Chapter 11
    FAQs about Auto Accident Insurance in Oregon 51

Chapter 12
    Insurance Company Tricks 55
        How Social Media Can Hurt Your Case 58

Chapter 13
    Independent Medical Exams 61

Chapter 14
    The Personal Injury Process – A Checklist 63

Chapter 15
Attitude is Everything 67

Chapter 16
Do I Need An Attorney to Settle My Case? 69

APPENDICES

Appendix A
What to Look For in a Personal Injury Attorney 71
Will I Get More Money if I Hire a Lawyer? 73

Appendix B
Settlement Lawyer or Trial Lawyer? 75
Client Bill of Rights 76

Appendix C
How to Find Good Doctors 77
Why We Generally Don't Take Medical Malpractice Cases 78

Glossary of Terms 79

Authors' Bios
Joshua Shulman 87
Sean DuBois 89
Our Firm: Shulman DuBois LLC 91

Afterword 93

Foreword

Who Should Read This Book?

This book is specially written for people who have been injured in Oregon. While much of the information contained in our book may apply in other states, personal injury laws vary greatly by state so please be sure to get the information for the state in which your accident occurred. Otherwise, you might not have the correct information and could jeopardize your own case.

While this book primarily addresses car accidents, people who have been injured in other types of accidents (construction, truck accidents, bicycle and motorcycle accidents, etc.) should also read this book to educate themselves about the steps and options for getting compensation. This book is a great tool to begin understanding the personal injury process.

Why Should I Read This Book?

Getting injured in an accident can change your life. On top of being hurt, you're probably confused, overwhelmed, and worried that insurance companies will not approve your claim and you will be left to deal with the bills. As if it weren't bad enough being injured, insurance company representatives can be confusing, belittling, insulting, and tricky. That's why you should read this book before you talk with the insurance company.

This book will help you understand the personal injury claims process. And if you understand the process, you will be better equipped to decide whether to negotiate with the insurance company for compensation yourself, or hire a lawyer. If you negotiate your claim yourself, this book will help you avoid common mistakes, and will give you important, helpful information that the insurance adjuster will not tell you. And if you do decide to hire a lawyer, the appendices will give you a much better idea of what to look for and what to expect.

Legal Disclaimer

(You knew it was coming!)

This book is not legal advice. We are not your lawyers.
"Legal advice" means advice that is given to you specifically, tailored to your situation, taking into account unique details of your particular claim. **Every case is different. This book will give you useful information, but it is general information.** There is no way we can give you legal advice without knowing the details of your case.

If you want legal advice, or if you want to create an attorney-client relationship, you must contact a lawyer and form a direct relationship with that lawyer. This is almost always done by signing a contract with that lawyer, in which you agree to hire the lawyer, and the lawyer agrees to represent you.

You cannot create an attorney-client relationship by reading a book. If, after reading this book and doing all of your research, you decide to hire a lawyer, you can call a personal injury law office like ours to make an appointment and sign an agreement, after which you will have an attorney-client relationship.

Finally, laws can change, and often do. Before counting on any law cited in this book, check it yourself or get a lawyer to check it for you. Although we have tried our best to ensure that all information contained in this book is up to date and relevant, Oregon laws are available at www.leg.state.or.us/ors/home.html.

Chapter 1

Seven Common Mistakes That Can Wreck Your Oregon Accident Case

Mistake 1: Giving a statement to the other driver's insurance company.

You may have to give a statement to your own insurance company, but giving a recorded statement to the other insurance company is an early Christmas gift to them—all tied up with a pretty little bow. Insurance companies will use that recording for one purpose, and one purpose only: to reduce the amount of money they pay you.

It happens all the time.

In one instance, a woman was hurt at work, and the case took three years to go to court. At trial, the opposing lawyer asked her, "Which way did you turn when you came out of the elevator?"

She answered, "I turned left."

The lawyer asked, "Are you sure you turned left, and not right?"

"Oh yes. Absolutely sure."

"OK, and just to be crystal clear, you are telling us that you are absolutely, positively, 100% sure that you turned left when you came out of that elevator?"

"Yes!"

He then played a tape of her conversation with the insurance company just a few days after the incident, when she was still in the hospital. On the tape, she said she turned right out of the elevator. Although seemingly inconsequential, this mistake led the jury to lose confidence in the accuracy of her testimony. She lost her case.

At trial, an injured person cannot play the recorded statement given to the insurance company. The Rules of Evidence only allow it to be used to contradict things the injured person says at trial.

A recorded statement cannot help you; it can only hurt you. So, while your own insurance company can require it of you, the other driver's insurance adjuster (called the "adverse insurance adjuster") cannot – and while they might try to trick you into giving a recorded statement, we usually advise our clients to avoid doing so, for their own sakes. **See Chapter 12 for Insurance Adjuster Tricks.**

"Should I Give a Recorded Statement?"

Here are 10 questions to ask the insurance company adjuster who wants you to "just sign a few forms" or give a statement. Usually, the insurance adjuster for the person who hit you will not answer these questions at all, but if they do, we will be surprised.

1. Will you admit in writing that the accident was not my fault?
2. How much insurance does the person who hit me have?
3. Will you give me a copy of the recorded statement that you have already taken from the person who caused this accident?
4. Will you promise in writing to give me a copy of any statements you get from witnesses?
5. If I sign your medical release, will you put in writing that you will immediately give me a copy of everything that you get using my signed release?

> 6. How much money have you set aside in reserves for my claim?
> 7. Have you done any video surveillance of me?
> 8. Will you promise in writing that you will not do any video surveillance of me or that you will tell me before you do?
> 9. What financial information have you already obtained about me?
> 10. Which of my neighbors have you already interviewed?

Mistake 2: Waiting to seek medical treatment, or not following your doctor's orders.

When you are in a car crash, your own insurance will pay all of your medical bills for a year after the crash, up to at least $15,000. This is called "personal injury protection" or PIP, and every Oregon auto policy is required to have this coverage. **See Chapter 7 for more on PIP.**

Neither the insurance company nor a jury will simply take your word for how injured you are. They are more likely to believe your doctor. But your doctor will not know how badly you have been injured unless you get the treatment you need.

The severity of an injury is judged largely by how much treatment you receive.

Imagine two people: Julie and Martin.

They both get the exact same injury: a broken ankle. They both go to the emergency room, then to an orthopedic specialist who puts on a cast. They both wear the cast for four weeks then get it taken off. After that, their stories diverge.

Julie goes to physical therapy twice a week for several months. She does her home exercises twice a day, according to her doctor's orders. She never misses an appointment. After five months of this, she's as good as new. So six months after she broke her ankle, she's right back where she was before the accident. She can ride a bike and jog just like she used to.

Martin, on the other hand, doesn't much like his physical therapist, and has trouble getting time off from work to go. So his ankle doesn't really get better. He goes to an appointment now and then, but doesn't do the exercises because he doesn't feel like they help, and he doesn't have the time! A year after the accident, his ankle still gives him trouble occasionally. He's almost better, but after a long bike ride it'll hurt, and he can't really jog anymore.

Who do you think will get more compensation for their injury? In our experience, Julie will get more. Jurors and insurance adjusters both will judge Martin harshly. They will be of the opinion that he would have gotten better if he'd tried harder – and why should they help him with compensation if he won't help himself by going to the doctor?

Don't ever avoid treatment because you think you'll get more money if your injury is worse. The reverse is usually true. Plus, in addition to probably getting more money, Julie's ankle is completely healed – which is more important than the money anyway.

A gap in treatment can also significantly lower the value of your case. If you went to physical therapy twice a week in January and February, then did not go at all in March, then went twice a week in April and May, jurors will be suspicious. Sometimes there is a good reason for this. But if your reason is, "I got sick of driving all that way and had other things to do," then you will be lowering the value of your case.

Get all the medical care you need, and follow your doctors' orders. This will show everyone concerned that you are serious about recovering from your injury, and your injury claim will often be taken more seriously as well.

Mistake 3: Lying to your doctor . . . or to anyone else.

If you have been injured and there is a possibility you may bring a lawsuit, you must be absolutely honest. No lies. No exaggerations. The insurance companies have huge databases, and they will spend some time researching your injuries and case if it will help them avoid having to pay you. They will find medical records that you don't even remember. They may interview your neighbors, friends, co-workers, and even your ex-husband or ex-wife. They may follow you around with a video camera. You simply cannot get away with lying, nor should you try.

If you plan to lie because you think you will get more money, no honest lawyer will want to work with you. We know there are dishonest lawyers out there, but we encourage everyone to find a lawyer who can get compensation for clients without resorting to tricks and deceit. If you ever have a lawyer ask you to lie, please report that lawyer to the Oregon State Bar.

For example, maybe you were an avid gardener before your accident and you spent many hours each weekend in your garden, and now you are reduced to taking a stool outside and clipping flowers for a few minutes before the pain stops you. You might be tempted to say, "I can't garden anymore." But then the insurance company could show a videotape of you sitting on your stool clipping flowers, and you look like a liar. It's better to say, "I can't garden for 10 hours a week like I used to. Now I can only sit on a stool and clip flowers." A moderate injury will not force you to completely stop doing an activity; the injury just makes it much harder.

Now, most people do not intend to lie, but exaggerating or even understating your injuries can hurt your case. So when you bring a personal injury case, you must be 100% honest with your doctors, with your lawyer (if you have one), and with the other side (whom you should not talk to at all without your lawyer there). The insurance company may not be honest with you – that makes no difference. The insurance company adjuster is not going to be on trial. You are.

The most valuable resource in your case is your credibility. If you lose that, you will lose your case.

Mistake 4: Going to a bad doctor.

The value of your case depends on many factors, but two of the most important are: your credibility, and how serious your injuries are.

Now, how does a jury (or a lawyer, or an insurance adjuster) figure out how injured you really are? Usually, the best way is to read your medical records and talk with your doctor. So the value of your claim lies mostly with you and your doctors. **For what to look for in a good medical provider, please see Appendix C.**

We hear about doctors all the time from our clients. Most of our clients love their doctors. But a significant number of clients hate them. If you hate your doctor, find another one! We know it's difficult, a hassle, and time-consuming, but it is so important that you trust your doctor. If you don't, then you will avoid making appointments, avoid keeping them when you do make them, and you'll be less likely to follow your doctor's orders. Remember, failing to maintain consistent treatments and not following your doctor's orders is Mistake #2.

Finding good doctor recommendations can be difficult, but take the trouble early, and get to a doctor you trust. Ask friends for recommendations, and search the Internet. If you do have a lawyer, that can usually be a good source for a recommendation as well, since personal injury lawyers work with lots of doctors.

It is a mistake to stay with a doctor you don't trust. And it can hurt your case if they are not credible. So find the right doctor for you, and this will make going through treatments, and eventually getting medical records and trustworthy medical opinions, that much easier down the road.

A good doctor who is well trained in injury recovery and case management is a huge asset. Often a well-trained doctor – whether a chiropractor, physical therapist, or other – is one of the key ingredients in successful recovery from an injury. Make sure that any doctor you see performs appropriate imaging studies, conducts regular re-examinations, keeps you informed of your progress, and refers you to specialists when that will be helpful for your recovery.

Mistake 5: Not preserving evidence or documenting damages.

If you are in a car crash that causes over $1,500 in damage to any vehicle, or causes any injuries, you are required to fill out a DMV report. Keep a copy for your records, as the DMV will not give you a copy later. You are also required to inform law enforcement about your accident, if it meets those criteria.

In an accident involving a serious injury, there can be a race to get evidence. The area should be photographed extensively. Skid marks should be photographed and measured. The automobiles should be photographed before they are moved. Most cell phones have cameras these days. Now is a good time to learn how to use it.

If you are receiving prompt medical care, it is usually not necessary to photograph your injuries. However, if medical records will not adequately preserve evidence of any injury, it is sometimes advisable to photograph it. In certain cases, the vehicles should be saved as evidence. Both medical records and photos can be extremely useful in showing liability and damages months later, when you might have forgotten the details.

If you have been seriously injured, you may not be in a position to take photographs. The best solution is for you to hire an experienced private investigator to document the evidence. If that's not possible, you may want to ask a relative or friend to document the scene and the damages for you, though you should be aware that this could sometimes look biased if the case goes to trial. If you can afford a professional, experienced private investigator, that is by far the best course of action. If you hire an attorney, the attorney will be able to hire a private investigator for you, as well.

If an accident was caused or made worse by a missing road sign, or a sign that is obscured by a tree or bush that should have been pruned, or any other road hazard, this should be documented immediately as it might be cause to sue a public body, in which case you have less time to file than if you are just pursuing damages from another driver's insurance. **See Chapter 4 for more information on Time Limits For Filing.**

Mistake 6: Not telling your lawyer about other injuries and accidents.

If you hire a lawyer, or are considering hiring a lawyer, for your personal injury claim, it is important to recognize that this will become a long-term, important relationship. This means you need to be honest and open with your attorney at all times.

Here are several things your attorney will need to know during your case:

<u>Your Criminal History</u>

Usually, minor unrelated incidents will not be relevant to your case – but you might not be able to recognize what's relevant or not, and your attorney can, so it's important to share this information.

Prior Injuries and Accidents

Opposing counsel will look for anything that might have caused your injuries before the accident, so that they won't have to pay your medical bills. If you do have any pre-existing conditions, your attorney will need to prove these were either made worse by the accident, or are unrelated.

Injuries After the Accident

If you get hurt after the accident, these costs will need to be separated from the costs for the injuries sustained by the accident – and even then the opposing counsel will probably try to claim your treatments stem from this second injury, not the first. So you need to discuss this with your lawyer and your doctors.

Bankruptcy

When you file for bankruptcy before your lawsuit is settled, the damages claim can become part of the bankruptcy estate. But an experienced personal injury attorney might be able to work with your bankruptcy attorney to try and see that as much of the money as possible goes to you and not to your creditors.

Divorce

If you're filing for divorce during a lawsuit, your spouse might be entitled to some of the money you will receive in your settlement. Talk to your lawyer about this to ensure that he or she can make decisions with this information in mind.

Your lawyer's job is to tell the best possible story, taking into account all of the facts. If your lawyer does not have all the facts, then your lawyer will not be able to tell a complete story. If your case gets to a jury, they will see the holes in your story and will not trust you. And juries do not give money to people they do not trust.

Mistake 7: Having low UIM coverage.

If your injury is worth $300,000, but the person who caused your injury only has $25,000 of insurance, all of our advice about telling the truth, and seeing a good doctor will not matter. You are probably only going to get $25,000, unless you have good underinsured motorist coverage (UIM). In Oregon, every driver is required to have at least $25,000 in UIM coverage, and if the at-fault driver's insurance limits will not cover your injuries caused by the accident, you can file a claim against your own insurance company for the difference. In some cases, even the UIM limits will not be enough to cover all your bills.

So, read Chapter 8 on UIM. Then call your insurance agent and ask for higher UIM limits on your policy. It is worth the money. It may be too late for this injury, but you can be prepared for the future.

If you have high UIM coverage, make sure your lawyer knows how to get that money for you. Any competent personal injury lawyer will know how to do that, but there are plenty of generalist lawyers who may not know how.

Car Crash or Car Accident?

Insurance companies love to talk about "accidents," because that word implies that your injury was nobody's fault. Insurance company lawyers like to use the word "accident" because they hope the jury will start to believe that the "accident" was not anybody's fault. In reality, an "accident" is usually caused by someone who wasn't paying attention.

In casual conversation, we call them "accidents" too, because that's how people talk. But when we're talking to a jury, or an insurance adjuster, we prefer to call them "car crashes" or "wrecks," or "collisions," because it turns out that, usually, they *were* somebody's fault. When we are talking among friends, this language does not matter much, and in this book, we will use every one of these phrases. But when we are in front of a jury, the choice of words can matter a lot. If you have been in a collision, you might start noticing that you get different reactions from people if you call it a "crash" than if you call it an "accident."

Chapter 2

7 Common Myths You May Have Heard from Friends, Relatives, or Well-Meaning Neighbors

1) MYTH
You need a lawyer for every accident.

TRUTH

Absolutely not. Many accidents do not require a lawyer at all. You may end up with more money in your pocket if you settle the case yourself. **But only if you understand the process.** Our goal in writing this book is to help you do that.

If you've done some negotiating before (and almost everyone has – with your boss, your spouse, your parents, or your children), use those skills here. You should use whatever negotiating tactic has worked for you in the past. For some people, that'll mean being nice and sweet and trying to connect with the insurance adjuster on a personal level – don't be afraid to ask about their children or their hobbies. But if you're more comfortable being businesslike, then do that. The key in negotiating is to do it in a way that *you're* comfortable with. Because working in a way that makes you comfortable will help you project confidence, which is always helpful in these situations.

We also recommend writing down your key points ahead of time, so that you can refer to them when you talk to the adjuster. In negotiation, it always pays to prepare as thoroughly as possible.

Adjusters have supervisors. If you're not making headway with your adjuster, ask to speak to her supervisor. Don't be rude about it, because most supervisors will start out wanting to protect their adjuster – you'll have to be able to explain to the supervisor why it wasn't working out with the adjuster.

Finally, please read this book thoroughly, as it will point out some of the common mistakes that people sometimes make. If you can avoid making those mistakes, you might not need a lawyer to make a successful injury claim.

2) MYTH

You have just hit the jackpot by getting injured. This is the "lawsuit lottery!" You will be buying a new car and a Hawaiian vacation with the money you get from the insurance company.

TRUTH

The purpose of the legal system is to compensate a person who was injured by someone else's carelessness. The purpose is not to make an injured person rich. This happens very rarely—if ever. Most of the multimillion-dollar cases you read about either (a) are not entirely true, (b) had the verdicts radically reduced by the judge, or (c) the amount of money awarded was the amount actually needed by the injured person. (You know how much medical care costs; if a person has been paralyzed and now requires round-the-clock care for a lifetime, $5 million probably will not cover it).

If someone has injured you, then his or her insurance company should pay the amount of money necessary to make up for what you have lost. But the law does not entitle you to more than that. **If you are looking to get rich quick, you will be sorely disappointed.** If you are looking for fairness and justice, you might, with a lot of hard work, get what you deserve. Remember, the adjusters will look at medical records and property damages and other finite numbers when making an offer – you cannot make unreasonable demands without the adjusters realizing they are unreasonable.

3) MYTH
You should call your insurance company right away after an accident and tell them everything.

TRUTH
Although you should call your insurance company to report the accident, **there are things you should not say to the at-fault driver's insurance company.** Remember, this is an adversarial process. The insurance company is not going to tell you anything that will help you. You should not tell them anything that will help them to pay you less money than you deserve. You may not lie to them! But that does not mean that you have to volunteer information that doesn't help you. And it doesn't mean you have to answer every question they ask. If the other driver (the one who caused the crash) hasn't answered all the questions asked by your representative (or by you), then why would you answer all the questions asked by that person's representative?

4) MYTH
You should get a fast settlement.

TRUTH
Actually, it's easy to get a fast settlement. What's unusual is a fast **and fair** settlement. The insurance companies love fast settlements, because if you are in a rush, they know they will be able to settle for pennies on the dollar. But if you want to get the full amount that your claim is worth, it is rare to get it quickly. Some cases, from accident to payment, can take years.

After the accident, you will need to contact your insurance company. Then, if you decide to pursue the case yourself, you will need to provide proof of medical treatments and eventually, after you are medically stable (which can take months), you will need to contact the at-fault person's insurance company and negotiate the amount you will receive for damages. All of this can take a while, especially if the adjuster is being difficult and delays or denies your claim. **See Chapter 12 for Insurance Adjuster Tricks.**

5) MYTH
You can never get a fair settlement in less than 90 days.

TRUTH

On rare occasions, you can get the full value of your case quickly. It generally happens in a "policy limits" case. This means that your case is clearly worth more than the limit of the insurance policy of the person who injured you.

For example, we recently represented a woman who was hit by a car while she was crossing a crosswalk on foot. She suffered a badly broken ankle, which required emergency surgery to place pins and rods to hold the bone in place. The person who hit her had $250,000 worth of insurance coverage, and since we were able to convince the insurer that the case was worth more than that, they paid the entire $250,000 within about 60 days. But this happened only because the value of the injuries was greater than the value of the insurance policy. And since the policy limit is the most the insurance company will ever have to pay, taking it quickly can be a good idea.

But before you take that policy limit settlement, make sure you are not leaving additional money on the table. For example, if the person has an umbrella policy, or was on the job for a company with an additional insurance policy, or if the person is wealthy, there might be other options you can pursue to ensure you are fully compensated for your injuries. **See Chapters 5, 6, and 8 for more information on "policy limits" cases.**

6) MYTH

If the person who hurt you has only $25,000 of insurance coverage, then that is all the money you can get.

TRUTH

This is sometimes true, but there are important exceptions. You may be entitled to get more money under your own insurance. This is called "underinsured motorist coverage," or UIM. If you do not have at least $250,000 of UIM coverage, or if you are not sure what this means, **read Chapter 8 for more on UIM.**

It is also possible to collect money directly from the person who hit you. The fact that a person has insurance does not mean you cannot collect from the person individually.

For example, if a jury decides that your injuries are worth $60,000, and the person who hit you only has $25,000 of insurance, then you can try to collect the extra $35,000 directly from the person who hit you. If that person is wealthy, this can be an excellent strategy. But if that person is broke, it will be a complete waste of time.

To know whether this is a useful strategy, you will have to figure out if the person who hit you has substantial assets. This is not always easy, but you can do it using a private investigator or an asset affidavit.

The McDonald's Coffee Case—Myth #7 Explained

There seems to be more and more criticism of personal injury lawsuits. People have tried to claim compensation for some very frivolous injuries. We hate frivolous lawsuits more than anyone. We make our living pursuing justice in the courts, and frivolous lawsuits give the courts and justice a bad name. Most personal injury suits are not only valid – they are the only way to ensure that insurance companies and bad drivers are held accountable, and good people are able to pay their medical bills.

The McDonald's Coffee case is one of the most famous personal injury lawsuits, but it is commonly misunderstood. People think they know all about the McDonald's coffee case. But there are some facts that are not widely known, that might change your opinion of the verdict. Was the lawsuit frivolous? Here are the facts. You decide.

Stella Liebeck was in the passenger seat of her grandson's car. She was 79 years old. After picking up coffee at a drive-through window, her grandson pulled over and came to a complete stop so Ms. Liebeck could open the lid to add cream and sugar. She was not driving, and the car was not moving. As she removed the lid, she spilled the entire cup into her lap.

- She received third-degree burns over 6% of her skin, and lesser burns over 16% of her body.
- She was hospitalized for eight days, and required skin grafts and debridement (medical removal of dead tissue).
- Two years of treatment followed.
- Ms. Liebeck asked McDonald's to settle the claim for $20,000, but they refused.

- During trial preparation, McDonald's admitted to more than 700 similar claims over the past 10 years.
- McDonald's admitted that it held coffee at between 180 and 190 degrees. Coffee served at home is usually 135 to 140 degrees.
- A few days before trial, the judge ordered both sides to attend mediation. The mediator, a retired judge, recommended that McDonald's settle for $225,000. The company refused again.
- At trial, a thermodynamics expert testified that if the coffee had been served at 155 degrees or less, Ms. Liebeck would have avoided serious burns.
- The Shriners' Burn Institute had published warnings to the fast food industry that they were unnecessarily causing serious burns by serving beverages above 130 degrees.
- A McDonald's executive who testified for McDonald's at the trial said McDonald's knew its coffee could cause serious burns, but had made the decision not to lower the temperature or to warn customers about it.
- The jury awarded Ms. Liebeck $200,000 to make up for her burns. But they also decided she was 20% at fault, so they took away 20% of that money.
- The jury also awarded $2.7 million in punitive damages, which equals about two days of McDonald's coffee sales. (In Oregon, the state keeps 70% of punitive damages. **See Chapter 3 for details.**)
- The judge then reduced the $2.7 million to $480,000, which is equal to about eight hours of McDonald's coffee sales.

- Finally, Ms. Liebeck settled with McDonald's in a confidential deal, so we will never know how much McDonald's ended up paying, though it has been reported to be less than $600,000.

Punitive damages in large cases like this are meant to punish the company for failing to protect consumers. **The facts of this case are a great example of how the media has spun some lawsuits to appear frivolous when they are actually legitimate claims with serious injuries.** As personal injury lawyers, we hope to combat this negative view of lawsuits so that injury victims do not ever have to face this "frivolous lawsuit" stigma.

Chapter 3

What Is My Case Worth?

What is a broken arm worth? How about a bulging vertebral disc that causes nerve pain down the arm for six months until surgery fixes it? What if the surgery doesn't work?

Unfortunately, there is no science to this. In fact, here's the crazy way that our society figures out what a broken arm is worth: we drag twelve people away from their work and their families, make them sit in uncomfortable chairs in a courtroom, force them to listen to a bunch of witnesses tell their stories, then lock the twelve people in a room and don't let them come out until they've decided how much that broken arm is worth. Letting a jury decide might seem strange, but it is a system designed to be fair to all parties involved. And I can't think of a better way. Can you?

Because each trial will have a different jury, it is impossible to say with any absolutes how much a personal injury claim will be "worth."

Of course, over 95% of cases never go to a jury. We, as lawyers, decide how much those are worth by trying to figure out what a jury would say. We look at other "similar" cases in the past, see what juries awarded in those, and make our best estimate based on every detail we know about the situation, the medical records, any laws that apply, the personalities and histories of the people involved, the evidence regarding whose fault the accident was, the policy limits, and so forth. If you decide to pursue your case yourself, you will need to do the same.

But because, during a trial, the value is decided by twelve human beings, with all the flaws and prejudices that human beings have, there is a whole lot more to be taken into account than just the injury. How much the jury likes you will matter a whole lot. How much they like your witnesses will matter too. And how much they like the person who hit you. The judge has a tremendous amount of discretion, and the judge's rulings can affect a trial. How good your doctors are at teaching a jury matters a lot. What the police report says matters.

In fact, so very many things matter, that it's really not possible to figure out what a case is worth until an extensive investigation has been done. But of course, there are guidelines. Here's one: **your case is probably worth less than you think, but more than the insurance adjuster is willing to pay.**

Even though a book cannot tell you what your specific case is worth, we can educate you about the different kinds of "damages." Damages is a vague term that helps us encompass all possible types of compensatory money an injury victim might receive from a claim.

In Oregon, there are two basic kinds of damages you can recover for a personal injury case: (1) "economic damages" and (2) "noneconomic damages." These used to be called "general damages" and "special damages," and you will sometimes still hear lawyers use these words. But the proper terms are "economic" and "noneconomic" damages.

Economic damages refers to the compensation you can get for any money you have lost due to the collision. Examples include:

- Money to repair your car, or the full value of the car if it was totaled
- Money to pay for medical bills
- Lost income if you were not able to work because of your injuries
- Money to pay for household services like cleaning and childcare if you were not able to do these things because of your injuries
- Money to compensate for future economic losses

Noneconomic damages are often called "pain and suffering." Noneconomic damages cover such things as:

- Pain
- Humiliation
- Mental suffering
- Emotional distress
- Inconvenience
- Interference with normal activities
- Damage to a person's reputation
- Aggravation to a previous injury

There are also **punitive damages**, which are meant purely to punish the wrongdoer. However, the State of Oregon takes 70% of any punitive damages. Then your lawyer will typically take 20%, leaving you with only 10%. This is then taxable, so you might end up with only about 5% of punitive damages. In the right case, it can make sense to try to get punitive damages, but most injured people are better off seeking only economic and noneconomic damages, which are usually not taxable in personal injury cases, under Internal Revenue Code 104(a)(2).

How Bankruptcy Can Affect Your Personal Injury Case

If you are in bankruptcy, or might be soon, this can have an enormous effect on any recovery you may get from a personal injury case. If you are in bankruptcy, your claim does not belong to you; it belongs to your bankruptcy trustee. Generally, you can keep up to $10,000. But the rest usually goes to your creditors. This is general information; there are plenty of exceptions, and negotiation is often possible.

If you are in bankruptcy, it is essential that you tell your bankruptcy attorney or trustee about any possible personal injury claim. If you hide a personal injury claim from your bankruptcy trustee, you would be committing fraud. You could forfeit any money you win, your personal injury lawsuit could be thrown out of court, and you could even go to jail. A good bankruptcy attorney can refer you to a personal injury attorney, and vice versa, and the two can work together to find the best solutions for you.

Chapter 4

"How Long Do I Have to File?" Oregon's Statutes of Limitations

You may have heard the saying that every American has a right to his or her day in court. What you may not know is that this "right" is subject to time limits that are sometimes confusing, and always strictly enforced.

The Oregon State Bar puts out a 247-page book called "Oregon Statutory Time Limitations." Those 247 pages are only enough to *summarize* the time-limit laws in Oregon. This is a complex field. There are many different limits for different types of situations. The only way to be absolutely sure of the time limit is either to do the legal research yourself, or have a lawyer do it for you.

Keeping firmly in mind that every situation is different, and that this book cannot give legal advice, this section will discuss the most common time limits. If you have been in a straightforward accident in Oregon, chances are these rules apply. But we cannot guarantee it.

In general, Oregon personal injury cases must be filed with the court **within two years** of the date of the injury. This does not mean you can decide one year and eleven months after your accident that you want to file – there is a lot of preparation that goes into filing a complaint. In general, attorneys prefer to take a case at least a year before the statute of limitations date. If you are pursuing your case yourself, you probably want to start the process at least a year in advance because you will not be as familiar with the steps required. **See Chapter 14 for more about the Personal Injury Process.**

Please be aware that the two-year time limit for filing a personal injury lawsuit is Oregon-specific. The time limits are different in Washington and California.

This can sometimes be extended by the "discovery rule." The discovery rule generally will not apply in accident cases, but it is something to be aware of for other types of injury. The discovery rule allows a person to start counting from the date the cause of the injury is (or should have been) discovered, rather than from the date of the injury itself.

Warning! Protect Your Rights!
Statutes of Limitations You NEED to Know

If a child is injured, the statute of limitations is complicated:
ORS 12.160 states that the time for bringing the lawsuit does not start being counted until the child turns 18. However, the time limit will never be extended for more than five years, nor will it be extended for more than one year after the child's 18th birthday. ORS 12.160 is available online at http://www.leg.state.or.us/ors/012.html. In general, if a child is 17 or older at the time of the accident, the statute will run in two years, just like for an adult. If the child is between 12 and 17, the time limit will run out on the child's 19th birthday. If the child is under 12, the time will run out 7 years after the injury.

If you were hurt by a drunk driver:
Special time limits apply. It is sometimes possible to sue the bar (or other establishment, like restaurant or nightclub)

that served alcohol to the drunk driver. This is only possible in certain circumstances, but to maintain even the possibility of such a suit, you must send a Dram Shop Notice (ORS 471.565) to the bar **within 180 days of the accident**. A Dram Shop Notice is a special letter that tells the establishment or person who served the alcohol that a claim for damages is being made against the establishment, a description of the time, place, and circumstances giving rise to the claim, and the name and mailing address of the person making the claim. If the drunk driving led to not just an injury, but death, then you have a year instead of 180 days.

Note: 180 days is not 6 months. There is no leeway in these time limits. ORS 471.565 gives the details, and is available online at http://www.leg.state.or.us/ors/471.html.

If you were hurt by a state, county, or city worker: You will have to file a Tort Claim Notice **within 180 days**. You must send the notice to the right person, and must say the right things. Details are in ORS 30.275, which is available online at http://www.leg.state.or.us/ors/030.html. The Tort Claim Notice has to say the same things that a Dram Shop Notice has to say: that a claim is being made against the public body, or an officer, employee, or agent of the public body; a description of the time, place and circumstances giving rise to the claim, and the name and address of the person making the claim. And again, if the result was not just injury, but death, then you have a year instead of 180 days.

If a person is killed in an accident:
The case is not an injury case, it is referred to as a "wrongful death" case, and many special rules apply. The time limit for filing a lawsuit in a wrongful death case in Oregon is three years from the date of the event that ultimately caused the death.

Remember, though, if a drunk driver, or a state, county, or city worker caused the wrongful death, you only have one year to file a claim.

If the last day of your time limit falls on a Saturday, Sunday, or court holiday, you have until the next court day. This does NOT apply to the 180-day Tort Claim or Dram Shop limits. Every once in a while, Multnomah County courts deal with budget shortfalls by closing on Fridays. Because that is not a Saturday, Sunday, or "holiday," it is not clear whether a due date of Friday would be stretched to the following Monday. Do not take that chance.

An experienced lawyer will not wait until the last day, the last week, or even last the six months to file a lawsuit – it takes more time than that to be truly prepared. You should not wait this long either. In addition to getting dangerously close to the time limit for filing a lawsuit, there are several other reasons why waiting can be detrimental to your case. Witnesses will have forgotten things. Evidence will be lost. And if you do decide at the last minute you do want a lawyer, most of them won't take the case if the Statue of Limitations date is too close. Do not wait until the last minute!

Chapter 5

Auto Insurance Policies – The Basics

If you've been in an accident, you will find yourself fielding calls, letters, and bills from multiple insurance companies. You may get confused, talking to the other driver's insurance company, thinking it's your own. It's easy to make mistakes, and to feel overwhelmed. We hope that laying out the different types of insurance will help you to stay organized.

Commonly, there is your automobile insurance, the automobile insurance for the driver who hit you, and your health insurance. There may be workers' compensation insurance, or disability insurance, as well. When a person dies from an accident, life insurance may come into play. Sometimes Medicare, Medicaid, or the Oregon Health Plan applies. Things can get complicated fast.

We cannot cover every type of insurance in this book. There are hundreds of insurance companies registered with the State of Oregon and licensed to provide insurance. But we will cover the basics of the most common types of insurance an accident victim typically has to confront after a collision.

You have car insurance—or should. It provides liability insurance, personal injury protection, and uninsured/underinsured motorist coverage.

Liability insurance means that if you hit someone else, and it is your fault, your insurance will provide a lawyer to defend you. They will pay any settlement or judgment up to $25,000, or more if you have paid higher premiums to get additional coverage. If you were in a crash that was someone else's fault, then you will be negotiating with their liability insurance. **See Chapter 6 for more on liability insurance.**

Personal injury protection, usually called "PIP," means your auto insurance will pay all of your medical bills for one year up to $15,000, or more if you have paid higher premiums to get additional coverage, as long as the medical care is for an injury you received while using a car. **See Chapter 7 for more on PIP.**

Underinsured Motorist coverage, known as UIM, is designed to provide money for you and your family if the person who hit you does not have any insurance, or does not have enough insurance to pay for all your injuries. **See Chapter 8 for more on UIM.**

Umbrella policies. Sometimes the person who hit you will have low auto insurance policy limits, but will have an "umbrella policy" that will pay additional amounts. Umbrella policies are usually large, often over $1 million. Before you ever take a settlement for the "policy limit" of a person's auto insurance, make sure to find out whether an umbrella or other policy may apply.

If you have been in a car accident, you will generally have at least two insurance companies to contend with: the insurance company for the person who hit you and your own insurance company's PIP department. **The PIP department is supposed to be on your side, but this isn't always the case.** If you have been paying your premiums, they should pay all of your medical bills up to $15,000 without much trouble. You will have to cooperate with them, which includes filling out some forms and giving them permission to see your medical records. This is so they know what they are paying for.

The insurance company of the person who hit you, on the other hand, is not on your side. The insurance adjuster *should* make you a fair offer, pay it, and let you go on your way. Unfortunately, many of them act as if their job is to hold onto that money with the tightest fist they can manage. **Read more about Insurance Adjusters in Chapter 12.**

The following chapters will discuss liability insurance, PIP and UIM in more detail.

Other Types of Insurance That May Apply

You will have to negotiate with any insurance that may cover you. These may include, for example:

- Medicaid / Oregon Health Plan
- Medicare
- Social Security
- Disability insurance
- Workers' compensation

If you are covered by workers' compensation for the injury you received, it may take some clever maneuvering to maximize your compensation. Often, with workers' compensation, you will be severely limited in the amount of compensation you can receive for your injuries.

We cannot write about all of the possible types of insurance you may run into, but we will say this: If you are covered by any of these insurers, and you decide to hire a lawyer, make sure the lawyer knows how to handle the particular type of insurance you hold. Otherwise, you may end up owing the insurance companies money after your settlement without even being aware of it. **Please see Chapter 10 for more about Medical Liens.**

In the case of disability or Medicaid, you could lose your coverage by surpassing their income guidelines. This can often be avoided by careful planning, but it must be done correctly.

Chapter 6

Liability Insurance

Every driver in Oregon is required to have liability insurance. Liability insurance is meant to protect you if you are legally responsible for an automobile accident.

If you are driving and hurt someone else, your liability insurance will provide you with a lawyer, and will pay the injured person whatever amount he or she is entitled to, up to your "policy limit" if you are found to be liable. You will not need to pay this attorney – your insurance company will pay their fees for you, from the premiums you have already been paying. This is one of the benefits that you get from the premiums you have been paying to your insurer all these years.

Your contract with your liability insurance allows the insurer to control the litigation. Sometimes they may make litigation decisions you do not agree with. They have the right to do that.

The law says your liability insurance has to take good care of you. They have to look out for you and your interests. For example, if someone is threatening to sue you for $40,000, and your policy limit is $25,000, your insurer has a responsibility to do what it can to try to settle the case for only $25,000. This is so you do not have to pay the extra $15,000 out of your own pocket.

When a liability insurer does not take good care of the person they are insuring, that person sometimes sues his or her own liability insurer. That is called a "bad faith" claim, because the person believes that the insurance company did not treat him or her honestly and fairly.

If you have been hurt by a person driving a car, you will usually be dealing with his or her liability insurance. If you decide to hire a lawyer, your attorney will deal with the other driver's insurance company's attorney for you.

Insurance Policy Limits

Every insurance policy has limits. This is the maximum amount that the insurance company will have to pay. Automobile insurance limits are typically quoted as two numbers with a slash between them. For example, as of this writing, ORS 806.070 requires that an automobile policy issued in Oregon must have liability limits of at least $25,000 / $50,000.

The first number is the most that the insurance company has to pay *to any one person* in an accident. So if the person who hit you has $25,000 / $50,000 limits, then his or her insurance company will never have to pay you more than $25,000 for your injuries.

The second number is the maximum amount the insurance company will ever have to pay *for the accident*. So if three people were hurt in the crash, the company would never have to pay more than $25,000 to any one person, but they also would never have to pay more than $50,000 for all three people combined. Which means that each person could get less than $25,000. If the person runs into a bus and injures 50 people, each one may get an average of only $1,000 each, because the insurer never has to pay more than the $50,000 for the entire accident.

Chapter 7

Personal Injury Protection – PIP

When you bought your insurance policy, if you are like most people in Oregon, you were thinking you were getting liability coverage, so if you caused a crash and injured someone, your insurance would take care of them. But your insurance also contains "personal injury protection," known as PIP.

The idea behind PIP is that if you get injured from "the use, occupancy or maintenance, of any motor vehicle" (ORS 742.520 (2)(a)), then your own insurance will pay up to $15,000 (as of this writing) for your medical treatment. If you have paid extra premiums for higher limits, then you may have more than $15,000 in coverage. They will only pay for medical treatment received within one year after the accident, no matter how much or how little of the $15,000 you have spent.

If you are hit by a car as a pedestrian or a bicyclist, and do not have car insurance, you may still have PIP, because there are circumstances in which the PIP for the driver who hit you has to pay your bills.

What PIP Pays

PIP is the first place to go to get your medical bills paid after any injury involving a car. In fact, when your health insurer finds out you were injured in a car crash, they usually will not pay your bills, because they expect PIP to pay them, up to $15,000.

PIP can make a huge difference in your life, particularly if you have no health insurance. But even if you do have health insurance,

PIP has no deductibles or copayments, and, within reason, **you can go to any medical provider you want**. Some PIP policies have a deductible, but Oregon law does not allow the deductible to be more than $250.

If you have been hurt in a car crash and you have auto insurance, use that PIP to get all the medical care you need.

Wage Loss

PIP will also pay some of your wage loss, but not all of it. PIP will pay 70% of your normal wages up to a maximum of $3,000 per month. One of the reasons they only pay 70% of your income is that, generally speaking, you do not have to pay taxes on the money you receive from PIP.

But there is a catch. PIP will only pay your wage loss if you miss at least 14 consecutive days of work. To collect wage loss reimbursement from PIP, you need a note from a doctor saying you cannot work for 14 days or more. And you have to miss at least 14 days of work in a row.

People often want to know, "If I use my vacation days or my sick days so that I am not actually losing my wages, can I still get PIP to pay my wage loss?" The answer is, "Sort of."

You can get PIP to pay your wage loss, but if you have used vacation pay or sick days, then the money PIP pays for wages lost is probably going to go to your employer, not to you. Then you would need to negotiate with your employer to get the sick days or the vacation days put back into your account in exchange for the PIP money you have given back to your employer.

If you do not generally work for pay—for example if you are a stay-at-home mom or dad—there is a PIP "wage loss" for you too. If, because of your vehicle-related injuries, you are unable to perform normal household functions (cooking, cleaning, childcare) for 14 days or more, PIP will pay up to $30 per day for you to hire someone to do these things for you. True, $30 doesn't usually cover the help you need, but it is better than nothing.

How to Get PIP to Pay

To get PIP benefits, you have to cooperate with your insurance company. This means you will need to sign a medical release, which allows them to get your medical records and speak with your doctors to find out if you are really injured. You will probably have to answer some additional questions for them as well. Some insurance companies will require you to give a recorded statement. This can be dangerous territory. If you are thinking of getting a lawyer, you should do that before you give anyone a recorded statement. **See Chapter 1 for more about why recorded statements are a bad idea.**

Chapter 8

Underinsured Motorist Insurance — UIM

When you bought your insurance policy, in addition to PIP and liability coverage, you also got UIM, which stands for "underinsured motorist" insurance. If someone else hits you and causes $150,000 worth of injuries, but only has $25,000 worth of insurance, UIM will make up the difference, but only if you have UIM policy limits of $150,000 or more. In Oregon, however, you are only required to have $25,000 of UIM coverage so most people only have the minimum.

UIM also includes coverage if you are hit by someone with no insurance at all. This is called "uninsured motorist" coverage, or UM. In an effort to simplify, we will group them all together and call it UIM.

If you have been hit by someone who does not have enough insurance to cover your injuries, you have three options.

Option 1: You can take the policy limit amount from the other driver's insurance ($25,000 in the above example). Plenty of people do that. Plenty of lawyers do that. It is a quick and easy solution.

Option 2: You can try to collect money directly from the person who hit you. If the person is rich, this may be a good way to go. But it is very difficult and expensive to collect money from most people. Even if you can get a judgment from the court against them, it can be expensive and time-consuming to garnish wages and attach bank accounts.

Generally speaking, when you try to get money from somebody who does not have much, you end up paying lawyers or collection agencies a lot of money, and you end up getting very little.

Option 3: Collect the $25,000 from the insurance company of the person who hit you, and then collect the rest from your own UIM coverage. This option is by far the best.

There is a catch. You have to have paid for this coverage. Your underinsured motorist coverage will only pay that additional $125,000 if you have paid for $150,000 or more of UIM coverage. You will also have to prove that your injuries are worth more than the $25,000 you have already been given. If your lawyer has already gotten you policy limits, however, much of the legwork has already been completed to establish a UIM claim.

If you have already been in a collision, it is too late to buy more underinsured motorist coverage for that collision.

But if you have not already been in a crash, or if you have been in a crash but you want to be better prepared in case you get in another one, you should purchase more underinsured motorist coverage. This coverage is cheaper than you might think. Rates vary, but one of the authors of this book is paying less than $40 extra every six months to have UM/UIM coverage of $250,000 / $500,000, instead of the minimum of $25,000 / $50,000.

If you do not have at least $250,000 of underinsured motorist coverage, stop reading this book, call your insurance agent, and ask what it would cost to get you up to $250,000 / $500,000 or more.

Seriously. Stop reading. Go call your insurance agent. Ask how much it will cost and write it down here:

$250,000 / $500,000 UM/UIM coverage for my family and me will cost me an extra $_____ every six months.

How Many Uninsured Drivers Are Out There?

- The Insurance Research Council conducted a study in 2009 that found about 10% of Oregon drivers (and one in seven drivers nationwide) were driving without insurance, and in January 2009 wrote, "approximately one in six drivers across the United States may be driving uninsured by 2010."
- The study also found that when the unemployment rate goes up, so does the rate of uninsured drivers.
- Most uninsured drivers do not have a lot of money, so if one of them hits you, the only money available to pay for your injuries is usually your own uninsured motorist coverage.

With one out of every six drivers out there driving without insurance, we strongly encourage you to protect yourself and your family by buying extra uninsured motorist coverage of at least $250,000 / $500,000.

Chapter 9

Health Insurance – Your Last Resort

Personal injury protection (PIP) is the first place to go to get your medical bills paid if you have been in a car crash. If you've been in a crash, call your own insurance company and speak to an adjuster about using your PIP for medical treatments.

PIP only pays $15,000 toward your medical bills, unless you have paid for higher coverage. Once that $15,000 is gone, your health insurance will have to start paying. And PIP only pays for one year, so if you need treatment for more than one year, you will need to be under your health insurance, even if you have not yet surpassed the $15,000. There are additional circumstances where PIP may not pay, and in such cases, you will need to rely on your health insurance.

If you have to use your health insurance to pay medical bills from a car crash, you may be in for a shock. Almost every health insurance policy in Oregon has a clause in it that you are probably unaware of. The clause is usually written in mind-numbing legalese, but the meaning is something like this: **"If you are hurt in an accident, and the accident is someone else's fault, and you get money for that accident from the person who hit you, then you will have to pay us back for all the medical care that we paid for because of that accident."**

With all the premiums you have been paying for your health insurance, you would think they would have to pay for your medical care when you have been injured. As it turns out, that payment is often just a loan, because your health insurer will put a lien on your case. **Please see more about Medical Liens in the next chapter.**

This is a shameful situation that should be corrected. Nonetheless, it is Oregon law. Almost all health insurance policies have this clause written in the contract that you signed when you bought your health insurance policy. You need to be aware that if you are in an accident and your health insurance pays $20,000 toward your medical care for your accident, and then later you get $50,000 from the insurance company of the person who hit you, your health insurance company is going to want its $20,000 back.

A good lawyer can often negotiate with your health insurance company and get them to reduce that amount, so that they collect less than the full amount they paid. But you are going to have to pay them back something, and if you do not negotiate hard, you are going to have to pay them back every penny.

Chapter 10

Medical Liens and the Importance of Negotiation

If your health insurance or your auto insurance (PIP) pays your medical bills due to an injury that was someone else's fault, and then you get a settlement from that person (or their insurance company), then your insurance company (that paid your medical bills) has the legal right to get back the money they paid for your medical treatment. They can do this by "lien" or by "subrogation." Their legal right to do this is in ORS 742.534, 742.536, and 742.538.

"Subrogation." Wikipedia has a definition: "circumstances in which an insurance company tries to recoup expenses for a claim it paid out when another party should have been responsible for paying at least a portion of that claim."

Here's our definition: when your health insurer (or auto insurer, or Medicare, or other insurer) steals your money.

In our opinion, this is an outrage. You have been paying insurance premiums so they would pay your medical bills, not so they would give you a loan. But it's the law, and you need to be aware of this flawed system because it can significantly affect your financial situation.

Often, the insurance companies will work out the payment among themselves without involving you. But sometimes they will force you to pay the lien.

Your best action is to first try to get them to work it out themselves. Encourage your own insurance company to get reimbursement from the insurance company of the person who hurt you.

If that doesn't work, the next best option is to negotiate the amount of the lien. Insurers will often reduce the amount you owe them if you negotiate well. For example, if they paid out $130,000 in medical bills, you may be able to talk them into accepting $80,000 or even less in full satisfaction of that money. In this negotiation, ORS 742.536 can be helpful, because it states that the insurance company should automatically reduce its lien by the percentage of your attorney fees and costs, which means that they normally reduce their lien by about 35%.

Even if you don't have a lawyer, they may still be willing to make this reduction, though they would not be legally obligated to. But be aware that many health insurers believe that because they operate nationwide, they do not have to abide by Oregon law. So those insurers may not be willing to automatically reduce the lien. But they may still be open to a good argument about why they should reduce the amount they are collecting.

When you are negotiating, just remember, vinegar works, but honey often works better. A strong argument about fairness is often surprisingly effective in getting them to reduce their lien. You may even want to remind them about some of the fine sentiments they probably have on their websites about how their mission is to help people in need.

In Washington State, and in California, if you're not "made whole" by your settlement, then you don't have to pay off the insurer. There's no subrogation until after an accident victim has been fully compensated. Oregon doesn't have that rule. **In Oregon, the health insurer can take your premiums every month for decades, then take all your money from a settlement.** They have the right to leave you without a penny if that's what their subrogation "rights" allow them to do.

It's a bad situation when you receive a settlement that is barely adequate, only to find out that you have to give a bunch of it to another insurance company. But with good negotiation skills, you can at least minimize the damage.

Chapter 11

FAQs about Auto Accident Insurance in Oregon

1) What if the other driver was at fault, but doesn't have insurance? How will I pay my bills?

Well, to pay your bills initially, you will be able to use your PIP **(see chapter 7 for more information)**. But in addition to PIP, you also have other coverage in your policy to cover expenses over $15,000.

In Oregon, every driver is required to have at least $25,000 in underinsured/uninsured motorist (UIM) coverage. This means that if someone who does not have insurance hits you, you can try to get compensation from your own insurance company. Keep in mind that the insurance company only has to pay $25,000 if that's the maximum amount of coverage you paid for. We suggest getting higher UIM coverage, but you can **read more about UIM in Chapter 8.** For now, just know that in Oregon, if you have insurance, you have at least $25,000 in UIM coverage for bills.

2) What if I don't have car insurance?

If the accident was your fault, and you do not have insurance, the other driver can try to make a claim against any of your personal assets for their damages.

If the accident was the other driver's fault, you can contact their insurance company and ask to have them pay your bills. Unfortunately, if you do not have your own insurance, you do not have the benefit of personal injury protection (PIP), which would pay your bills initially until the other insurance company can begin paying. This means you may need to pay some of your bills out of pocket until the case is settled. **See Chapter 7 for more on PIP.**

If the collision was not your fault, and you were driving without insurance, you can still receive economic damages from the at-fault driver's insurance, but the law does not allow you to recover non-economic damages. That is your punishment for driving without insurance, even though the crash was not your fault.

3) You keep talking about car accidents. What if I was walking and got hit by a car? Do pedestrians get compensation?

Yes, they do! If you were hit by car, your accident is covered by the driver's car insurance. Which means that you can file a personal injury claim with their insurance just like you would if you were hit while in your car. It is the same for bicyclists – if you are hit by a car while riding your bike, you can file a claim for compensation with the driver's insurance company.

In addition, if you are walking or bicycling, and you are injured (but do not have health insurance) the at-fault driver's PIP will be available for you to use for initial medical expenses.

4) If someone else is driving my car, like one of my kids, does my insurance cover their injuries if someone hits them?

Yes, your children and anyone else who drives your car are covered under your insurance policy. This means that PIP will pay their bills, and that UIM coverage will be available if the at-fault driver's insurance does not cover the injuries, property damages, and wage losses.

5) If my car is totaled, but I still owed money on it, will my insurance pay off the note?

Unfortunately, they might not. It depends on how much you still owe on the car. The insurance company only has to pay the "actual cash value" of the car, which means the amount it would cost to replace your car with one in similar condition. They will examine your car's mileage, previous damage, tire wear, etc. to determine the actual cash value, but if you owe more money than this amount, you will not be compensated.

If your car is not totaled, however, and the insurance company only pays for repairs, you can file a diminished value claim as well. A diminished value claim, if successful, will compensate you for the loss in value to your car. For example, if you have a new car and another driver hits you, even if you get the car repaired the accident will have lowered the value of your new car – you can ask the insurance company to pay this difference in value.

6) I carpool. If I get into an accident, will my car be covered?

Yes, as long as you are not using your car to carpool for profit, your car is covered. For example, if you carpool to work, all your passengers are covered by your insurance policy. But, since you will be responsible for their injuries if you cause an accident, you may want to increase your liability coverage since you have more passengers. Just in case.

7) What if I'm driving someone else's car?

If you are not at fault, you're fine – the at-fault driver's insurance will cover your expenses and the damages. If you are at fault, then damages will probably be paid by the vehicle owner's insurance. Be aware, however, that if they are not insured or are underinsured, you could be held responsible financially. Your own auto insurance should apply, though.

8) What about motorcycle accidents?

If you are in a motorcycle accident, pretty much all the same rules apply. You are responsible for damages if you are found to be at fault, but you can be compensated if the other person is at fault. Motorcycle policies are not required by law to include PIP, and they usually don't. We recommend you pay extra to get PIP coverage.

9) The person who hit me was driving a company car. Can I sue the company?

Probably. You might be able to sue the company *if* the driver was using the car for company business. For example, if a construction company truck was being driven to a job site, the company might be liable. If the construction company employee was just driving the car on his own errands, his own auto insurance policy may need to cover the costs. Actually, in a case like this, you might want the company to be responsible for the damages because policy limits are usually higher for commercial vehicles.

Chapter 12

Insurance Company Tricks

You should definitely communicate with your own insurance company's adjuster, but the insurance adjuster for the other driver's insurance will probably be more difficult to deal with. Here are some of the tricks the insurance adjuster will use to try and make you settle your case for an unfair amount.

1. Pretending To Be Your Friend.

This is the worst. Insurance companies are a big business, and they make money by denying your claim. They pay their adjusters to give you as little money as possible. The adjuster is on the opposite side from you. This may be a good person who coaches Little League, donates to charity, and loves dogs. But always remember: his job is to pay you as little money as possible. Don't buy it!

2. Delaying the Process.

Insurance companies handle millions of claims. If they can save $100 on each one, they increase their bottom line by hundreds of millions of dollars. They have a whole lot of money that they are investing, and they are making lots of money on those investments. Every day that they can delay paying you is a day that they can earn interest on their money. They also know that you are getting squeezed, and every day they can delay makes you just a little bit more desperate to settle.

3. Requiring Unnecessary Information.

This is just one more way for them to cause delay. If you've broken an arm in an accident, they'll ask for medical records from five years ago that have nothing to do with your arm. This is not right. You are only required to give them medical records related to the body parts that were injured in the accident. They don't need to read about your flu shots! But try telling that to the average adjuster. They just want more and more paper; even if it has nothing to do with your case. Because, who knows, maybe there will be something in those records that will help them fight your case. And even if not, delay is always good for them — and always bad for you.

4. Hiding Insurance.

Sometimes adjusters will tell you there's only $100,000 (or $300,000, or $25,000, or whatever their number is) of insurance. Then after a lawsuit has been filed, you find out there's an umbrella policy for $1,000,000. Let's just say we "strongly suspect" that they knew that when they told you there was only $100,000.

5. Breaking Promises.

We hear from people all the time who tell us that the adjuster made them a promise, and then broke it. *Get it in writing!* Many insurance adjusters are poorly trained, underpaid, overworked, or just plain don't care. These are not professionals who care about their reputations. If it's not in writing, it means nothing.

6. Acting Like Medical Experts.

I've never met an insurance adjuster who went to medical school. But they always seem to have opinions about your medical treatment. They think they know when you should be better, because their computer says that ten chiropractic treatments is too much for your injury.

7. Undervaluing Medical Bills.

Health insurance in the USA is complicated. Typically, a hospital or doctor may bill, say, $500, for a procedure. But the insurer, whether it's PIP or health insurance or Medicare, will only pay, say, $200. The doctor accepts that as full payment. But here's the question: if the insurance company of the person who hurt you is going to pay you for your medical bills, do they pay you $200 or $500? The answer is $500. That's the law in Oregon. But adjusters will often tell you they only have to pay $200. That's not right, but if you let them get away with it, then they just saved their shareholders $300 at your expense.

8. Not Taking Liens Into Account.

We've already talked about liens that your health insurance company might put on your case. Some insurance adjusters won't tell you about that when they're trying to settle with you. So they write you a check, and nobody tells you that you're going to have to turn around and pay that money to your health insurer, until it's too late. Whenever you settle your case, make sure you know what all the liens are. This includes PIP liens and health insurance liens.

If other insurance has been paying your bills (Oregon Health Plan, Medicare, anyone else), make sure you know the amount of their lien. Get it in writing, and take it into account before you settle.

How Social Media Can Hurt Your Claim

You might not have thought about this, but what is posted on social media sites like Facebook and Twitter can really (negatively) affect your personal injury case.

Example:

Defense Attorney: *"So, your injuries have kept you from doing your normal activities?"*

You, the Injury Victim: *"Yes, I can't do anything I used to do."*

Defense: *"And you used to garden regularly, but now you can't?"*

You: *"Correct."*

Defense: *"Can you tell me who this is gardening in this photo, taken by your daughter two months after your accident and posted to her Facebook account?"*

You: *"Me, but I was only out there for 10 minutes because...."* (interrupted)

Defense: *"I understand. Gardening must not be a 'normal activity.'* (sarcasm) *No further questions."*

As you can see, it is very important to monitor everything about your online presence.

Our suggestions:
1. Consider disabling or changing the privacy settings on your social media and blog accounts.
2. Google yourself. If you find anything that could affect your case, consider removing it.
3. Do not post anything about your accident, your injuries, your recovery, or your case. Ask your friends to refrain from doing so as well. This includes, pictures, comments, and videos.

Important Notes:
You must not destroy evidence. But you don't have to offer evidence to the entire world, either. Taking pictures off the Internet is not the same as destroying evidence. You are legally required to cooperate with the opposition in certain ways, but you certainly do not need to make their job easier by making evidence public.

Also, the fact that items, updates, blogs, etc., can be removed from the Internet does not mean you have the freedom to do whatever you want and just not post it online. You should not lie or attempt to conceal evidence. Remember, even with these new social media outlets, opposing counsel can still find out about your activities the old-fashioned way: by talking to family, friends, and doctors, and even by hiding in the bushes and videotaping you.

Chapter 13

Independent Medical Exams

In the last chapter, we discussed insurance adjuster tricks. But there is one trick that's so important we wanted to give it a separate chapter: **how adjusters can use an independent medical exam (IME) as an excuse to deny your injury claims.**

An independent medical examiner is a doctor who has not been involved in a patient's treatment and care, and is chosen by the insurance company. It's kind of like a second opinion for the insurance industry.

Although every case is different, it's generally not good if an accident victim has to see an IME. It usually means that the insurance company thinks the injured person is over-treating or is not really hurt or is not as seriously injured as they say. If a PIP independent medical examiner finds that the injured person has recovered, the insurance company stops paying the medical bills, and then you either have to pay for the medical treatment yourself or stop seeking treatment.

An IME, or independent medical exam, is performed by a doctor who has never previously treated the patient (or plaintiff) involved in a personal injury case. According to ORCP 44:

"When the physical condition ... of a ... person ... is in controversy, the court may order the party to submit to a physical ... examination by a physician. ... The order may be made only on motion for good cause shown and upon notice to the person to be examined and to all parties and shall specify the time, place, manner, conditions, and scope of the examination and the person or persons by whom it is to be made."

In English, that means that an "independent" medical exam can be used to determine if a patient is as hurt as he or she says. So an "independent" examiner is brought in for a kind of second opinion, if you will.

But there's a big problem with independent medical examiners: They're not really very independent at all. In fact, a lot of these "independent" medical examiners are quite dependent on the defense teams and insurance companies – and vice versa. As personal injury lawyers, we like to call this a DME, for "defense medical exam," because it's the defense that requests them, and it's the defense that benefits from them.

Although the doctors will not have worked with the patient before, they have almost certainly worked with the defense or insurance company, and will probably work with them again. The defense chooses the doctor and pays for the doctor. And that doctor often makes a decent amount of his or her income from the "independent" medical exams.

In general, the defense requests an IME with the hope that the doctor will come back with a diagnosis much more in line with what the defense wants to be said. And the doctors almost always do. What that usually boils down to is doctors performing short, poor exams, and then writing up a report that helps the defense, and hurts you.

It's important to know that IMEs can only be ordered by the court. If a defense wants an IME, it's only a request. Second, the defense must show "good cause," or a reason for the exam other than "I don't want to lose my case, so I'm bringing in another doctor who might take my side." Often, the defense believes it's their "right" to an IME, but they are sadly mistaken.

Chapter 14

The Personal Injury Process

Here is a checklist of some steps you'll want to consider in settling your case. Please note, this is **not** a list of what we do. As lawyers, we are able to take advantage of the legal system to do things differently. To write everything we do would not be helpful. This is a checklist of items that we hope the average person will find helpful. We can't guarantee that it's complete, because it's not! But we hope it will be useful to you.

You can find more detailed information about each of these items elsewhere in this book; this is just a checklist.

1. Preserve all evidence: take photos of the scene, interview witnesses, etc. Consider hiring a private investigator if the case is complicated or there is a question of liability.
2. **Get all the medical treatment you need.**
3. Check your PIP policy. Make sure PIP pays its full amount, which should be at least $15,000. You can ask for a PIP ledger to see how much money you have used, and how much is still available.
4. Check your health insurance policy. It should pay anything that PIP doesn't pay.
5. If your PIP adjuster wants to send you to an IME, decide whether it's worth going – it could create a medical record that can be used against you. You can decide it's better to refuse, even though then PIP will stop paying.
6. Find out the insurance policy limits of the person who caused your injury, including any umbrella policy.

7. If the policy limits are not enough to cover your compensation, perform an asset check on that person to find out if they can pay out of their own money above and beyond the insurance policy limits.
8. Read your UIM policy, and figure out whether you want to make a UIM claim as well. Typically, this can only be done if your UIM limit is higher than the liability limit of the person who hurt you, and your injuries warrant that much money.
9. If you have lost wages from the accident, document that carefully. You will probably need notes from doctors saying that you were not able to work, and a letter from your manager saying what dates you were unable to work and how much that cost you in wages. If you are self-employed, you'll probably need to pay an accountant or economist to write a report concluding how much money you lost due to the injury. If you have specific clients who cancelled orders due to your inability to work, get affidavits from them.
10. Decide whether your case can benefit from ORS 20.080 (see Chapter 16 for more information). This will limit you to $10,000 maximum recovery, but can be very motivational to insurance companies because they will usually also have to pay attorney fees.
11. Figure out if your PIP or health insurer (or anyone else who has paid your medical bills) will demand to be paid back out of your settlement. Will they have a lien? Get this in writing!
12. Consider whether publicity (or the threat of it) may be helpful in your particular case. If you are suing a company, for example, they will probably find the threat of publicity

dire enough to want to settle quickly so as to not hurt the business.
13. Get all of your medical records and original bills. Not the amounts actually paid, but the original bills. We suggest keeping these all organized in a binder or folder so you can reference them later.
14. You may wish to create a spreadsheet summarizing your injuries and medical treatment. If you do, it may be only for your use, or you may decide to give it to the other side to convince them to pay you more money.
15. Decide what evidence you want to give the insurer to convince them that the accident was not your fault, and that your injuries are real and were caused by the accident. You may want to save some evidence to tell them later on, to try to push up the negotiated settlement further along in the process. Decide now what evidence you're going to include, and what evidence, if any, you want to save for later.
16. Write a demand letter to the insurer. Include your medical bills and records. Include whatever evidence you've decided to give them up front. Give them a time limit in which to respond. Thirty days is usually enough, though it depends on the complexity of the accident and injuries. Make sure to take any liens into account. If you're using ORS 20.080, be sure to follow those rules closely, and have an attorney ready to file suit immediately if you don't receive an offer within the 30-day time limit.
17. Negotiate. Get everything in writing.
18. Negotiate with anyone who is claiming a lien on your case as well. Example: "I can settle this case for $15,000, but only if you'll agree to reduce your lien from $11,000 to

$6,000. Because if you don't reduce your lien, I'll only end up with $4,000."
19. If you are able to come to an agreement, then read the insurance company's release very carefully before signing it. It is binding.
20. Cash your check.
21. Pay back any liens, if necessary.

Chapter 15

Attitude is Everything

These are the times when you find out what you are really made of. Anyone can be optimistic when the sun is shining and the flowers are blooming. But we Oregonians know how to keep a good attitude when the weather is bad.

It is natural and easy to fall into self-pity when you have been hurt because someone else was careless. You have come face to face with the fact that the world is deeply unfair. As a result of your injury, you can no longer hold your new grandchild. You cannot care for your family. Your relationship with your husband or wife suffers. You feel helpless.

Let us be clear here. Any good lawyer will want to hear every single detail about how your accident and injuries affected your life. Every detail. Your lawyer will want to hear everything, including the whining – whining is honest. Your lawyer must be able to understand your injuries so well that he or she can describe them to the jury, so you don't have to. But once you've told your lawyer every detail, it's your lawyer's job to tell your story. **Your job will be to get on with your life, with as much hard work and optimism as you can muster.**

Let me tell you a story. It may be a myth. But it is a good story.

A boy was severely injured in a car crash. He suffered nerve damage, and could no longer walk. He was stuck in a wheelchair for the rest of his life. Eventually, he learned to "walk" 10 to 20 feet with two forearm-braced crutches.

By the time his case came to trial, he was 12 years old. Harvard doctors, Johns Hopkins doctors, and OHSU doctors all walked up to the witness stand, one after another, and told the jury that the boy would never walk again. The boy's mom came up and told the jury how much the boy used to love playing tag, climbing trees, playing baseball, but now he'd never run again. Dad talked about how much he had been looking forward to coaching his boy in Little League, but now he'd never play again. More medical specialists came up and told the jury the boy would never walk again.

Finally, the boy himself was called to the witness stand. His father pushed him to the witness stand in his wheelchair, and the boy started to get out with his crutches. The judge told him he could stay in his wheelchair, that he did not have to get up into the witness box. But the boy said no, he wanted to sit in the right place. The court clerk moved to help the boy up, but the boy waved him off. He struggled mightily with the help of his crutches to get out of his chair, up the step, and into the witness box. You could have heard a pin drop in that courtroom.

Finally, he got into the witness chair, and the bailiff swore him to tell the truth.

The boy's lawyer asked him one question: "Johnny, are you ever going to walk again?"

The boy's answer: "Absolutely!"

The insurance company lawyer did not cross-examine him; there was nothing to say. As the boy worked his way back out of the box and into his wheelchair, you could see the insurance company lawyer calculating how many millions of dollars that boy's winning attitude had just cost his company.

Chapter 16

Do I Need an Attorney to Settle My Case?

You may not need an attorney for your accident. If you have minor injuries, you are not in bankruptcy, all of your medical bills have been paid by PIP, and the insurance company treats you respectfully and truthfully, you may be better off settling your lawsuit directly with the insurance company.

It is usually difficult to find lawyers to take clients with minor injuries, so you may have no choice in the matter. There is an exception to this, though, in Oregon. Keep reading to learn more about your options.

How to Get a Lawyer for a Small Case – ORS 20.080

You can get a lawyer for any case you want—if you are willing to pay $300 or more per hour. But if you want a lawyer to work on a contingency basis, meaning that you pay nothing up front or out of pocket, and the lawyer takes a percentage of whatever he or she can get for you, it can be very hard to find a lawyer for a small case.

The insurance companies figured this out a long time ago and refused to pay more than a few hundred dollars on smaller cases, because they knew injured people could never get lawyers for those cases. Eventually, the Oregon Legislature figured out that insurance companies were not playing fair, and the Legislature enacted Oregon Revised Statute (ORS) 20.080.

ORS 20.080 makes it possible to find a lawyer for a case worth $10,000 or less. Under this law, if the insurance company refuses to make a reasonable offer within 30 days of receiving a certain type of demand letter, **the insurance company can be made to pay your damages AND your attorney fees!** This is basically a law meant to discourage insurance companies from taking advantage of people.

This law is complicated, and a full explanation is beyond the scope of this book. ORS 20.080 can be incredibly helpful if you've suffered injuries (but they do not make your case worth more than $10,000). Typically, this means that you did not break any bones, or suffer any permanent damage. Cases of whiplash that heal within a few months often fall into this category.

If you would like more information about this law, order our free report on ORS 20.080 at www.smallercase.com. Or call us at 503-222-4411 and ask for a free copy.

Like all laws, this one is subject to change. Check www.leg.state.or.us/ors/home.html for legal updates, or visit our website at www.pdxinjurylaw.com.

Appendix A

What to Look For in a Personal Injury Attorney

If you have decided to hire a lawyer, how do you find a good one? We can offer a few hard and fast rules, and a few guidelines.

Hard and Fast Rules

Rule #1: Meet with the lawyer before you sign anything. If you have a bad feeling about the lawyer, trust your gut instinct, and go elsewhere. You will have to tell your lawyer everything and be completely honest. It is very difficult to be completely open and honest with someone you do not trust.

Rule #2: Make sure your lawyer is willing to go to trial. If you do not get a reasonable offer, your lawyer needs to be able to tell you that, and then be able to do something about it.

Rule # 3: Make sure your lawyer explains all fees up front. You do not want any surprises.

Rule #4: Make sure your lawyer has adequate malpractice insurance. Even the best lawyers in the world are human, and anyone can make a mistake. One mark of a good lawyer is that he or she is prepared; a lawyer's mistake should not become the client's problem.

Legal malpractice insurance is meant to protect clients like you. If an attorney makes a mistake, and loses the client money to which they are entitled, this type of insurance will help to compensate the client for the loss. In other words, if the attorney messes up, the client can make a claim against the attorney and get some of the money the attorney lost them.

Every lawyer in Oregon is required to carry at least $300,000 in malpractice insurance. A careful lawyer will carry more than that. If your case is worth more than $300,000, you should be sure that your lawyer has enough malpractice insurance to cover you. Do not be afraid to ask your lawyer how much malpractice insurance he or she has.

Guidelines

Guideline #1: Take a look at the **Client Bill of Rights at the end of the next chapter.** Some of them may not be important to you. But decide which ones are important to you, and find a lawyer who agrees to abide by them.

Guideline #2: Specialists beat generalists. If your lawyer writes wills, secures adoptions, and does divorces, he or she may not understand the intricacies of injury law.

Guideline #3: Your lawyer should be a member of the Oregon Trial Lawyers Association (OTLA) and the American Association of Justice (AAJ). Membership in these organizations shows that your lawyer is proud of what he or she does, cares about justice, and is willing to put money and time toward the cause of justice.

Guideline #4: Ask around. If you can get a referral from someone you trust, that is an excellent place to start. But be aware, a lawyer who did a divorce or reviewed a real estate deal for a friend may not be the right lawyer for an injury case.

Guideline #5: If you want the personal touch, ask the lawyers you call how many cases they handle at a time.

Guideline #6: If you have a smaller case, educate yourself about ORS 20.080.

Guideline #7: Your lawyer should be licensed to practice in Oregon. An out-of-state lawyer will not be familiar with Oregon law. Out-of-state lawyers can try to settle Oregon cases, but if they have to file a lawsuit, they will probably have to join up with an Oregon lawyer, and they won't know Oregon law.

Guideline #8: Your attorney should educate you.

Guideline #9: Interview more than one attorney before you hire anyone.

Guideline #10: Beware of an attorney who rushes you into signing. Your lawyer should encourage you to take your time and make an informed decision.

Will I Get More Money if I Hire a lawyer?

There is no way for any lawyer to guarantee results in any case. But we can tell you that the insurance companies are very interested in this question, and have studied it. The Insurance Research Council issued a report called "Injuries in Auto Accidents: An Analysis of Insurance Claims." This report studied more than 87,000 auto injury claims.

The Insurance Research Council found that the average insurance payout to a person with a lawyer was more than 3.5 times higher than the average payout to a person without a lawyer.

Could this be why the insurance company tries so hard to convince you not to hire a lawyer?

Appendix B

Settlement Lawyer or Trial Lawyer?

Some lawyers advertise that they have been to trial hundreds of times. This may or may not be useful.

The lawyer may have done a lot of criminal trials. Criminal trials are very different from personal injury trials.

Some other lawyers may go to trial often because they are not very good at negotiating, so trial is the only way they can get full value for the case.

Some lawyers may go to trial often because they have so many cases they cannot tell them apart. If a lawyer has too many cases, he may go to trial more often. That lawyer may enjoy being in the courtroom so much that he does not put his full effort into getting the best possible offer before deciding to go to trial.

However, any of the above lawyers would be better for you than the lawyer who will never go to trial. In our opinion, a lawyer who accepts a personal injury case and then refuses to go to trial out of fear should not be allowed to practice law. The insurance companies know who these lawyers are, and they have a name for them: "settlement lawyers."

Of course, a lawyer should not be too eager either. But make absolutely sure that your lawyer is willing to go to trial. A settlement lawyer is not ready to take your case as far as it needs to go.

It may not matter so much how often your lawyer actually goes to trial. What matters is that your lawyer is *willing* to go to trial.

More than 95% of cases settle. Very few go to trial. But many cases are settled for far less than they are worth because the injured person's lawyer is fearful of going to trial and the insurance company knows it.

> **Client Bill of Rights**
>
> **What you should expect from a lawyer.**
> 1. You have the right to a lawyer who is enthusiastic and informed about you and your case.
> 2. You have the right to a lawyer whose staff is enthusiastic and informed about your case.
> 3. You have the right to a lawyer who turns off the phone, stops checking email, and focuses on your case.
> 4. You have the right to have your phone calls returned within 48 hours.
> 5. You have the right to a lawyer who is willing to take your case to trial if the insurance company will not make you a reasonable offer.
> 6. You have the right to be treated like a human being, not just another case.
> 7. You have the right to a lawyer who will be completely honest with you, and who will demand complete honesty from you.
> 8. You have the right to be kept informed about your case.
> 9. You have the right to a lawyer who will encourage you to ask questions, and who will take the time to answer them.
> 10. You have the right to have all fees and costs explained to you in detail, up front, so there are no surprises.

Appendix C

How to Find Good Doctors

We are not doctors, but we regularly work with people who are seeing medical doctors, naturopathic physicians, chiropractors, surgeons, acupuncturists, massage therapists, osteopaths, and all sorts of other medical providers and specialists. In our opinion, the most important things to look for are:

1. **Excellent medical skills.** Healing from your injuries is more important than your lawsuit, and must be your doctor's primary concern. It should be your primary concern too. Your health is more important than your lawsuit.
2. **Trustworthiness.** You must be able to trust your doctor. A doctor who has not earned your trust will not be able to help you as much as a doctor who you can confide in.
3. **Credibility and honesty**. A good doctor should be absolutely honest with you, and with everyone else he or she deals with. A doctor who just tells you what you want to hear is not what you should be looking for.
4. **Willingness (but not eagerness) to testify in your case if necessary.** Most doctors do not enjoy testifying. That is as it should be; they are busy healing people, and don't want to spend hours helping with a lawsuit. But your doctor's testimony will probably be the most important evidence you have in your lawsuit. If your doctor refuses to testify, it will make your case very difficult.

5. **Large referral network of specialists.** Your doctor should know many specialists, and should refer to them freely. Also, your doctor should not disparage other specialists, especially if those specialists are helping you. For example, if you are seeing both a physical therapist and a chiropractor, they should be willing to work together. If one of them says that the other is not helping, but you feel that they are both helping, then the one who is talking disparagingly about the other one is not being helpful in your healing process.

Why We Generally Don't Take Medical Malpractice Cases

We don't generally take medical malpractice cases because we believe that, in order to best serve our clients, it is important to maintain an excellent relationship with the doctors who treat our clients. And it is tough to maintain an excellent relationship with someone you have sued.

We will occasionally make an exception for an unusual situation, for example, truly egregious behavior by a doctor.

If you believe you have a case against a doctor for medical negligence, please give us a call. We know the best medical malpractice attorneys in Oregon, and we are happy to get you in touch with the right attorney for your particular issue.

Glossary of Terms That You May Hear During Your Claim

Action: Usually refers to a legal action or filing of a lawsuit, which begins the judicial process leading either to a dismissal, award, or settlement of the action.

Affidavit: A written statement affirmed or sworn by oath before a commissioner or a notary public for use as evidence in court. In Oregon we now often use Declarations instead.

Age of Majority: The age when a person acquires all the rights and responsibilities of being an adult, including the right to sign a contract and to file a lawsuit Minors cannot file lawsuits on their own, but must do so through a guardian of some kind. In Oregon, as in most states, the age is 18.

Allegation: Something that someone says happened, often stated by a plaintiff in the form of a complaint, or asserted by a defendant as a response to the plaintiff's complaint.

Alternative Dispute Resolution: Methods for resolving problems without going to court, such as mediation and arbitration.

Answer: The defendant's written response to the plaintiff's complaint.

Arbitration: A less formal trial. There is no jury, and the rules of evidence are relaxed.

Attorney Fee: The compensation a lawyer receives for legal services performed, in or out of court; can be an hourly rate, a flat rate, or a contingency fee. Most personal injury lawyers work on a contingency fee basis.

Breach of Warranty: When a retailer or manufacturer fails to follow through with a promise or claim about a product.

Civil Lawsuit: A lawsuit in which one does not need to prove criminal liability. In a criminal lawsuit, the State is trying to put someone in jail for breaking a law, and it must be proven beyond a reasonable doubt. In a civil lawsuit, an injured person is trying to get compensation for his or her injuries and it only needs to be shown to be "more likely than not."

Compensation: The monetary award transferred from defendant to plaintiff to make up for some wrong, damage, or injury caused by the defendant's actions or inaction.

Contingency Fee: Most lawyers are paid hourly, and the range is usually from $150/hr all the way up to $500/hr or more. But with a "contingent fee," you pay the lawyer nothing up front. There is no hourly fee. Instead, you pay the lawyer a percentage (usually 33% to 40%) of all money that the lawyer can get for you. If the lawyer cannot get you any money, you don't have to pay the lawyer's fees at all.

Crashworthiness: The measure of how well a vehicle withstands a crash. If a vehicle does not meet required standards, the faulty design can result in injury to occupants during a crash, and therefore a lawsuit against the manufacturer for not meeting those standards.

Damages: Has two different meanings. "Damages" can refer to the amount of money you have lost or to the suffering you have undergone as a result of your injury. How much you have been damaged. And "Damages" also refers to the amount of money allocated to compensate you.

Deposition: After a lawsuit is filed, the lawyer for either party may require the other party or independent witnesses to come to the lawyer's office and submit to a "deposition" under oath. The lawyer will ask the "deponent" (the person being questioned) questions about the case, to which the deponent must give a response. A court reporter will be present and write down all questions and answers. At trial, the lawyer might introduce the questions and answers into evidence, perhaps to show that a witness has changed his story from the story he told at the deposition.

Discovery: After a lawsuit is filed, each party is allowed to obtain information in the possession of the opposing party. This process is called "discovery." Discovery tools include the deposition, requests for admission, interrogatories (in Federal Court only; not allowed in Oregon State Court), and requests for documents.

Ex Parte: A legal proceeding in which only one side appears in court. Ex parte proceedings are usually allowed only when immediate action is necessary and there is not enough time to allow the other side to respond. And usually, despite this definition, the side that is appearing does actually have to give the other side notice.

Fiduciary: A person who is legally and ethically obligated to advance the interests of another person over his or her own interests. This term is usually associated with the type of duty a trustee owes to a beneficiary, and it is the duty a lawyer owes to his or her client.

Interrogatories: After a lawsuit is filed, either party may seek to "discover" information from the other party. One of the discovery tools is "written interrogatories," which ask the other party certain questions that must be answered in writing and is under penalty of perjury. These answers may be used against that party at trial. In Oregon, interrogatories are only allowed in Federal Court, not in State Court.

Law of the Case: If a judge makes a ruling on a legal issue during a case, it becomes the standard in that case and becomes binding throughout the life of that particular case.

Loss of Consortium: A legal claim for compensation for the loss of a marital or family relationship, usually in the form of love, companionship, community, and comfort.

Medical Malpractice: Improper or negligent treatment of a person under a medical professional's care, which results in harm to the patient.

Misrepresentation: False advertising, especially when ads claim that a product is safer than it truly is.

Negligence: Failure to exercise a reasonable degree of care, resulting in an unintended injury to another party and a needlessly technical term for carelessness.

Nursing Home Abuse: Any physical, sexual, verbal, psychological, or financial abuse perpetrated against residents of a residential care facility. Although nursing home abuse is a growing problem, many victims do not report violations because they are scared or ashamed.

Opinion: The legal reasoning relied upon by the court in rendering a judgment or decision on the matter before the court. Appellate opinions that are published are considered to be law and will serve as legal precedent for future cases.

Personal Injury Damages: Losses for which the law allows compensation. In personal injury cases this includes economic and non-economic damages, and sometimes punitive damages.

Preponderance of Evidence: What the plaintiff's burden is in a personal injury claim. Generally, this means proof, by more than 50%, that the defendant was legally responsible for an injury. This is much easier to prove than in a criminal case, which must be proven "beyond a reasonable doubt."

Product Liability Law: Law that holds manufacturers, wholesalers, and retailers responsible for the safety and quality of their products.

Punitive Damages: Money that is sought not to compensate the injured person, but to punish the wrongdoer. In Oregon, a person is not allowed to even ask for punitive damages until a judge has approved. And if a person gets punitive damages, the State of Oregon keeps 60% of it. The person then usually pays 20% to her lawyer, and then has to pay income tax on the remainder. This is why there are very few punitive damages verdicts in Oregon.

Rebuttal: Argument made in response to the other side's argument.

Request for Admissions: As part of the "discovery" process, either party to a lawsuit may serve on the other party written requests to admit certain facts, in order to save time at trial. Admissions will then be admitted into evidence at the trial.

Request for Production of Documents: As part of the "discovery" process, either party to a lawsuit may serve on the other party a written request for production of specified documents, such as medical records, driving history, insurance policies, photographs, repair records.

Rules of Evidence: Lawyers are not allowed to just say whatever they want at trial. They are limited by the rules of evidence to saying only things that are legally admissible. In theory, this is based on fairness, and on disallowing arguments that are based on emotion rather than facts. In practice, these rules are not always fair. For example, in an injury lawsuit, the jury is not allowed to hear whether the person who caused the injury has insurance – which can leave a jury under the impression that a sweet old lady will have to pay a verdict, when in fact it's her insurance that will have to pay damages.

Settlement: An agreement between two sides to end the case, usually by the defendant paying some money to the person who was harmed. The settlement can be in a lump sum or it can be structured into payments over a period of time by a third party.

Statute of Limitations: A law limiting the length of time a potential plaintiff has to file a lawsuit. These statutes vary depending on circumstances. In Oregon, they can be as short as 180 days in some cases.

Structured Settlement: An agreement in which one party agrees to pay the other a sum of money usually in the form of periodic payments over a period of time, as opposed to a lump sum payment. Property and casualty insurance companies often purchase annuities to pay the costs of such settlements.

Summary Judgment: A motion during litigation and prior to trial, where one party asks the court to rule in its favor without a trial.

Tort: Any action or failure to act that wrongs, damages, injures, or harms another, and thus forms the basis of a civil lawsuit.

Wrongful Death: A death that occurs because of someone else's malice, negligence, or recklessness.

Authors' Bios

Joshua Shulman

Portland attorney Joshua Shulman passed up his first opportunity to become a lawyer. As a senior at Reed College, he applied to law school, and while the application process was proceeding, took a position at a large corporate law firm in Boston. His experience there went so strongly against his values that he changed his mind about being a lawyer and withdrew his law school applications.

A few years later, following some travel and stints in organic farming and residential real estate, having returned to Portland with his wife to settle down and raise a family, Joshua also returned to the idea of practicing law. He realized being a lawyer didn't necessarily mean following the path that had turned him off initially—working for a firm representing faceless corporate entities and focusing on billable hours. He could practice in a way that was consistent with his values and passions—working for deserving individuals, where he could really make a difference in people's lives.

Joshua attended New York University School of Law, but spent his last year as a visiting student at Portland's own Lewis & Clark Law School to return to the city he loved so much. After graduating from law school, he became an executive at a Portland financial planning company that specialized in investing the funds of personal injury victims who had received large settlements. He saw firsthand what a difference that money made in the quality of care the clients were able to get and in their recovery overall. He also met many successful personal injury attorneys and was struck by how much the best of them cared for their clients.

Following that experience, he opened his own personal injury law practice and later formed a partnership with Sean DuBois, a like-minded attorney he met while volunteering on a committee for the Oregon Trial Lawyers Association (OTLA).

Joshua has been published in Trial Lawyer magazine, has served on the Publications Committee for OTLA, and is a writer for *The Huffington Post Blog* covering legal and national topics. He has given speeches on topics related to personal injury law, and is a member of Public Justice, Southern Poverty Law Center Leadership Council, the Oregon Trial Lawyers Association Guardians of Justice, American Association for Justice, the Oregon State Bar, Oregon Public Broadcasting, and is a proud graduate of Bill Barton's Litigation Boot Camp.

Outside of his law practice and related activities, Joshua enjoys spending time with his wife and two children, taking them to Little League, soccer, Kung Fu, and other activities, and gardening and growing fruit trees.

Sean DuBois

Some might say Sean DuBois was destined to be a lawyer. A successful competitive debater in high school, Sean attended college at the best debate school in the nation on a debate scholarship. On the fast track to a top law school, Sean began to see his friends burn out at big law firms helping rich corporations get richer. He decided to explore other options before committing to law school.

Sean decided to pursue his love of nature and the outdoors, spending the better part of a decade living as simply as he could all over the western United States and then in Hawaii and Florida, where he worked as a research diver at Florida Atlantic University's Department of Ocean Engineering. He saw up close how corporate greed and irresponsibility were ruining the naturally beautiful places he called home. It made him think more broadly about the need to protect people and the environment from the excesses of corporate power. He decided to return to his previous calling and use his skills to help individuals fight multibillion-dollar insurance companies and corporations.

Early in law school, Sean went to work for some of the best personal injury attorneys in Oregon. Following admittance to the Oregon State Bar, Sean worked with a well-known senior personal injury attorney in Portland, and then formed his own practice, DuBois Law Office. While volunteering on a committee for the Oregon Trial Lawyers Association (OTLA), he met Joshua Shulman, a local personal injury attorney with a similar passion for representing deserving individuals fighting for justice. They joined forces and formed Shulman DuBois LLC.

Sean is a dedicated and active member of OTLA, where he is a Guardian of Justice member, regularly serving on committees and actively participating in fundraising and political efforts to support civil justice. He has been published in *Trial Lawyer* magazine and actively supports other pro-civil justice movements such as the American Association for Justice and Trial Lawyers for Public Justice.

Sean and his family love living in the Pacific Northwest and often take advantage of the outdoor opportunities the area provides. Sean free dives and scuba dives on the Oregon Coast and he and his wife, Lena, along with their two elementary school-aged children ski together every chance they get. They also travel to Sweden, where Lena was born and raised, to visit her family as often as possible.

Our Firm: Shulman DuBois LLC

Our philosophy is Fewer Cases. Better Results.

We refuse to take so many cases that we cannot remember our clients' names. We refuse to fight the traffic downtown to work in an anonymous high-rise, choosing instead to work out of a converted bungalow in SE Portland.

We limit the number of cases we take so we can spend lots of time on the cases we do take. We enjoy working that way, and we believe that it gets better results for you. We turn down far more cases than we accept. **But if we do take your case, we guarantee that you and your case will get the time and attention you deserve.**

If you are looking for a lawyer, please remember – not all lawyers are created equal. We encourage you to find a lawyer that you feel comfortable with. We love our work. We believe this passion makes us better lawyers, but mostly we want to help injured Oregonians – if you need a referral, we can help with that as well. Call 503-222-4411 to start discussing your specific case.

Afterword

Congratulations! You now know a lot more than the average Oregonian about how to handle your personal injury case. You definitely know more than the insurance adjusters want you to know. You have educated yourself, and that is the best way to improve your chances of success.

Thank you for reading this book. We hope you found it helpful – we know the time after an accident can be extremely difficult. If you have any questions after reading this book, we invite you to call our office.

We encourage – nay, beg – our readers to tell us about anything that is unclear in our book. To call us with questions. To criticize. These critics have been instrumental in helping us make the third edition better than the second. Thank you to all of our critics, with the biggest thanks to the harshest critics.

To contact our office with questions, comments on the book, or for information about our legal representation, please call 503-222-4411. You can also visit our website and the Portland Personal Injury Resource Center at www.pdxinjurylaw.com.

~~IIII~~
~~IIII~~ Voicemail
    101 Sean
  < 102 Lena
    103 Eric
  Hold for CNx